Montessori Children's Center
of Allen Park
4141 Laurence St.
Allen Park, MI 48101
(313) 382-2777

Me ke aloha pumehana
L. R. McBride

about
Hawaii's
Volcanoes

about Hawaii's Volcanoes

by

L. R. McBride

Copyright 1967, 1972, 1977 & 1984 by
THE PETROGLYPH PRESS, LTD.

All rights reserved. No part of this book may be reproduced or transmitted in any form or by any means, electronic or mechanical, including photocopying, recording or by any information storage and retrieval system, without permission in writing from the Publisher.

Revised by Madame Pele
1985

ISBN 0-912180-00-5

18th Printing
December 1985

CONTENTS

	Page
Introduction	5
Kinds of Volcanoes	6
A Hawaiian Volcano	8
How the Volcanoes Erupt	10
Kinds of Lava	12
How the Hawaiian Islands Were Made	14
Hawaii Island	16
Mauna Loa Eruptions	18
Mauna Loa	19
Kilauea Volcano	22
The Latest Outbreak	29
Kilauea Iki Crater	32
Halemaumau	33
Kilauea Eruptions	35
The Hawaiian Volcano Observatory	37
Taking A Volcano's Temperature	38
How a Seismograph Works	39
When Is the Next Eruption?	41
Explosive Eruptions	42
Fossils	43
Hawaii Volcanoes National Park	45
Haleakala Volcano	47
Pele, the Volcano Goddess	48
About the Mt. Saint Helens Eruption	50

To the Mists of Paliuli

ABOUT HAWAII'S VOLCANOES

INTRODUCTION

The earth we live on has more than five hundred active volcanoes. There are also several thousand volcanoes that are either dormant (sleeping) or extinct (dead).

Usually when you think of a volcano, you imagine a steep-sided mountain with fire and smoke shooting out the top. Some volcanoes are not like that at all!

In some places in the world when a volcano erupts, the people have to leave the land in order to save their lives. When they come back, they find their farms and towns destroyed. Sometimes a volcano explodes without warning, and thousands of people and animals are killed.

The volcanoes in Hawaii are safe. You can visit them even when they are erupting.

KINDS OF VOLCANOES

There are three main kinds of volcanoes in the world. Each kind looks different and erupts differently too.

One kind is made of loose material and is called a cinder cone. The cinder is blown up in the air from a crack or hole in the ground and falls all around the place from which it comes out. The result is a volcano shaped like this. Cinder cones are often the smallest of volcanoes.

Another kind of volcano is made of melted rock that has cooled in many layers, one on top of another, like candle wax dripped on a table top. Because the melted rock moves a long way before it gets hard, it makes a rounded mountain like this. It is called a shield volcano. These are the largest volcanoes.

The third kind of volcano is made by erupting both cinders and melted rock. It is called a composite volcano. It looks like this. Most volcanoes in the world are of this type.

ABOUT HAWAII'S VOLCANOES

This is the volcano you often see in movies and read about in books. Sometimes composite volcanoes explode or pour out a fiery cloud that kills many people. Two thousand years ago, a city in Italy, called Pompeii, was buried by ash from such an eruption.

The volcanoes in Hawaii are shield volcanoes. They rarely explode, but erupt quietly. Usually, fountains of melted rock shoot up into the air, and the lava falls back to make molten streams and rivers that pour into a crater or flow slowly down the side of the mountain.

When a volcano in Hawaii erupts, thousands of people come to watch it. A man once wrote in a newspaper that seeing a Hawaiian eruption was like watching a bonfire, a steel mill and fireworks, all at the same time.

The old Hawaiian people called it *alealea,* the greatest of entertainment. Most of them were not afraid of eruptions. When a lava flow came down the mountain, they moved out of the way. When the lava was cold, they built their houses on it.

A HAWAIIAN VOLCANO

A model of a Hawaiian volcano looks like an unbaked pie with a thumbprint right in the middle of it.

The thumbprint is a flat-bottomed hole that is called a caldera.

The caldera may have a small hole in the bottom of it, like the one made by a pencil inside the thumbprint.  The small hole is called a crater.

A Hawaiian volcano has a design on the crust like a pie, too! This design is a line or weak place called a rift zone. It is marked with cracks and craters that have fallen in.

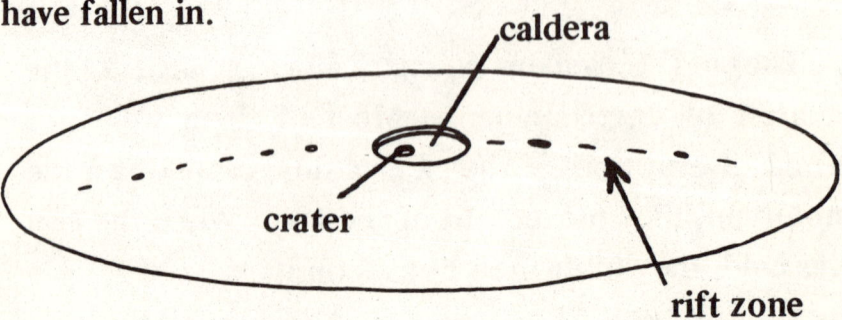

ABOUT HAWAII'S VOLCANOES

A pie has to have some holes or weak places in the crust. If it doesn't, when the pie is baked and some of the juice becomes steam, it could blow up all over the oven.

The rift zone on the volcano, like the design on a pie crust, makes the volcano safer. When the pressure inside becomes too great, it can leak out from many cracks and holes.

Just as the juice may bubble from a pie when it is baking, a Hawaiian volcano may erupt any place where the crust has a weak spot in it. Usually, an eruption happens in the caldera or along the rift zone.

When the eruption is in the caldera, the melted rock generally stays inside. It rarely overflows or runs down the side of the mountain. Along the rift zone, the melted rock that has been erupted may flow into a crater or down the volcano into the ocean.

When the hot lava meets the sea, the water boils around it, and steam may rise hundreds of feet into the air. When this happens, many fish are killed.

ABOUT HAWAII'S VOLCANOES

HOW THE VOLCANOES ERUPT

The melted rock rises from about thirty-five miles inside the earth and slowly fills up the spaces between the rocks under the crust of the volcano. This space is called the reservoir.

As the reservoir fills with melted rock, the crust of the volcano begins to rise or swell up, like blowing a little air into a big balloon. When there is enough pressure inside the reservoir, the crust cracks and the lava comes out.

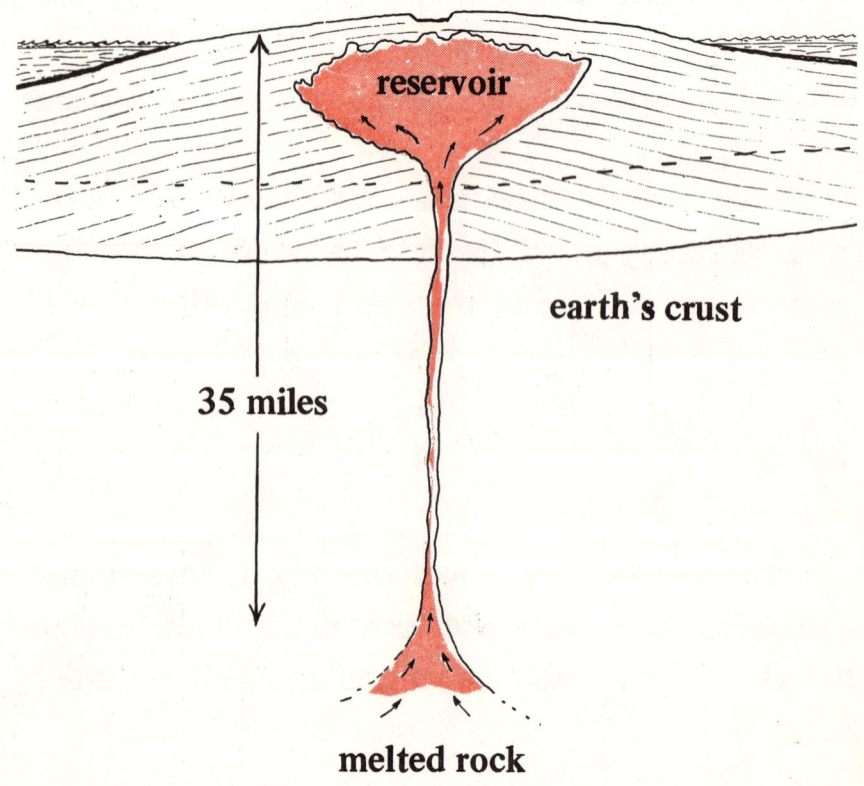

The melted rock is very hot, very fluid and has a lot of gas in it under pressure. As it comes out of the ground, the pressure becomes much less, and the gas expands suddenly. This causes the melted rock to squirt very high into the air. It makes a fountain like the one you get when you shake a bottle of "soda pop" with your thumb over the opening and then move your thumb off part way.

When the pressure goes down in the reservoir, the eruption stops, and the crust of the volcano sinks down again.

Sometimes, when a volcano eruption in the caldera ends, the top of the mountain seems to seal itself off. The melted rock keeps on rising into the reservoir. This time it is pushed into the cracks of the rift zone underground. Then, in a weak place, it erupts far down the mountain. An outbreak on the side of the volcano is called a flank eruption.

KINDS OF LAVA

There are two kinds of lava that come from eruptions of Hawaiian volcanoes - *pahoehoe* and *aa*. Both are the same kind of rock but look completely different.

Pahoehoe lava cools from the faster moving flows of melted rock. Because it is more fluid, the surface is smooth and glassy.

Sometimes the skin or crust of the lava wrinkles or pushes together, making a surface that looks like ropes laid side by side. More often, *pahoehoe* looks like rock pillows fitted together like a jigsaw puzzle. The center of a *pahoehoe* stream often remains fluid after the rest of the flow gets hard. Then, if the still melted part drains away, it leaves a tunnel, or lava tube.

ABOUT HAWAII'S VOLCANOES 13

Melted rock that is less fluid moves forward slowly and cools with a very rough surface. Hawaiians named this kind *aa*. A fast *aa* flow may move as much as one hundred feet in one hour.

Pahoehoe can flow thirty-five miles an hour down a steep slope. Often, where a *pahoehoe* flow slows down, as on a large, flat place, the edges of the flow become *aa*.

Where an *aa* flow pushes into the ocean, it makes the sea boil and steam. Some of the *aa* explodes into glassy black sand that washes along the shore. The most famous black sand beaches on Hawaii are Punaluu and Kalapana on the southern side of the island.

HOW THE HAWAIIAN ISLANDS WERE MADE

Perhaps during the time dinosaurs lived on earth, a great crack began to open on the floor of the Pacific Ocean. Three miles below the surface of the sea, melted rock began to flow from the crack, layer by layer. The first volcanoes of Hawaii were born! After a long time, some of the volcanoes grew high enough to push their tops above the ocean.

As soon as the first volcanoes stopped erupting, they began to be cut away by rain and ocean waves. Today, all that is left of some of them are coral reefs perched on the shoulders of old, dead volcanoes.

At the same time that the first volcanoes were dying, new ones were being built, as the great crack opened toward the southeast.

Today, there is a line of volcanoes almost two thousand miles long. The centers of the volcanoes seem to be evenly spaced about thirty miles apart. Their edges problably overlap each other like the rocks in a stone wall. Only a few of them are above the ocean.

ABOUT HAWAII'S VOLCANOES 15

The newer volcanoes above sea level make up the Hawaiian Islands. Hawaii, the big island, is the youngest island of them all. It is the only one that still has very active volcanoes.

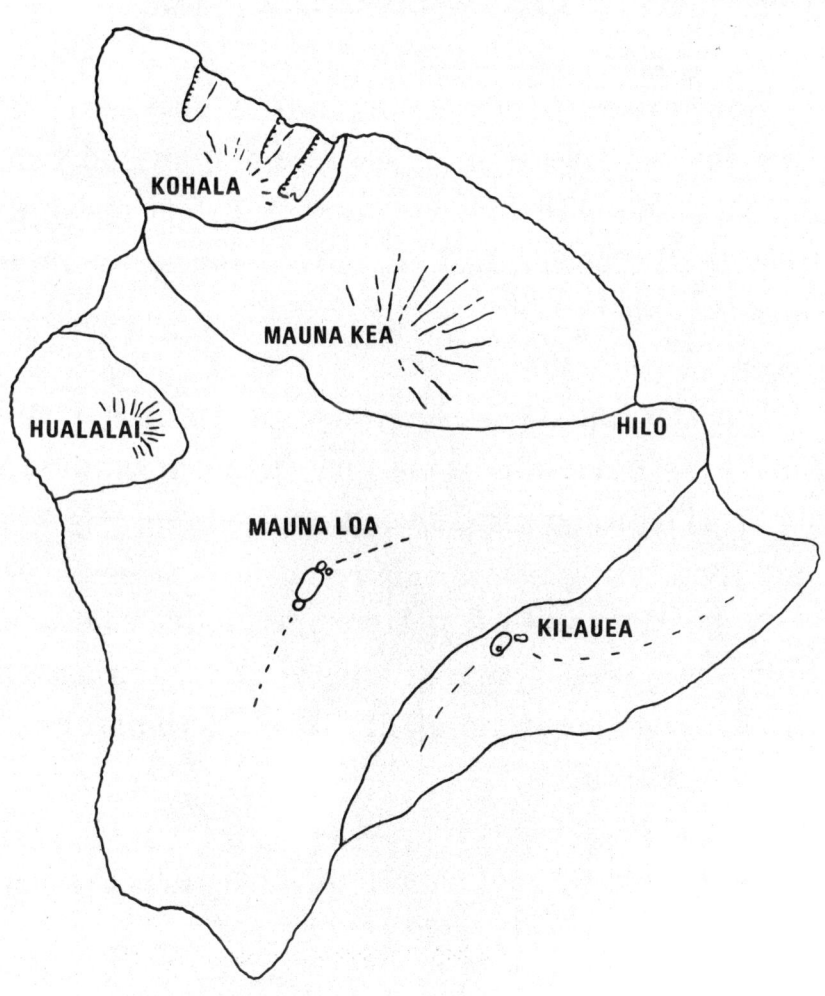

HOW HAWAII ISLAND WAS MADE

The island of Hawaii was made by five great volcanoes.

Kohala, the northern end of the island, is the oldest. It is covered with old cinder cones and has deep valleys cut into it on the windward side.

Mauna Kea (white mountain) is also very old. Probably it hasn't erupted for several thousand years. It stands more than thirty thousand feet above the floor of the ocean, making it the highest mountain in the world.

Hualalai, on the western side of the island, may have been quiet for a long time before it erupted in 1801. It hasn't erupted since then.

Mauna Loa and Kilauea are very active volcanoes. Both have been active as long as the Hawaiian can remember. They form all of the southern part of the island of Hawaii.

More will be said about them in the next part.

ABOUT HAWAII'S VOLCANOES

Other volcanoes continue the line toward the southeast. All of them are still below the surface of the ocean. Some of them are already big mountains standing more than two miles high above the ocean floor.

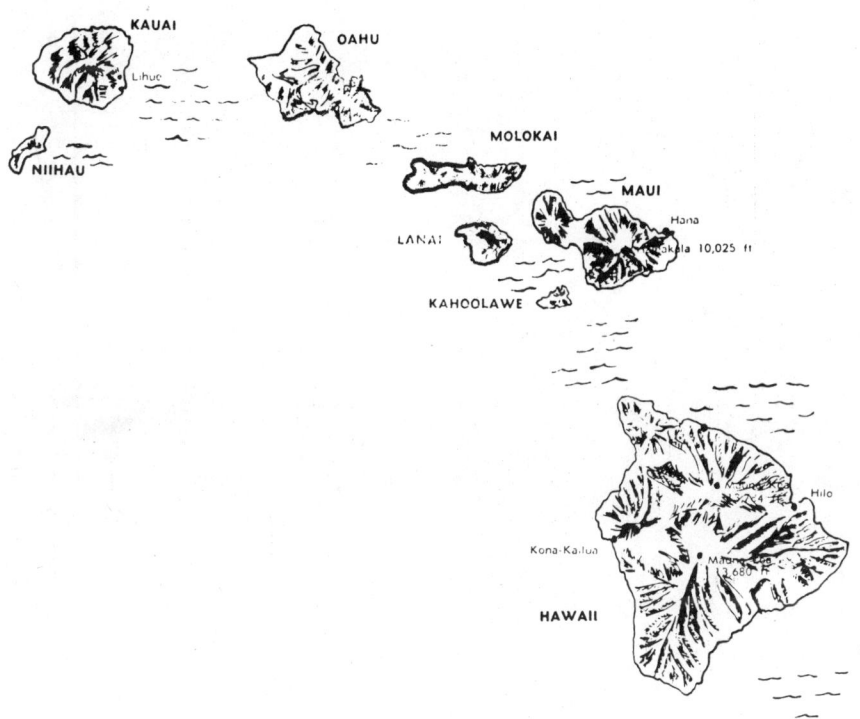

MAUNA LOA ERUPTIONS

YEAR	TOP	ON THE SIDE
1832	1	
1843	1	1
1849	1	
1851	1	
1852	1	1
1855	1	1
1859	1	
1865	1	1
1868	1	
1870	1	
1871	1	
1872	1	
1873	2	
1875	2	
1876	1	
1877	1	1
1880	1	1
1887		1

YEAR	TOP	ON THE SIDE
1892	1	
1896	1	
1899	1	1
1903	1	1
1907	1	
1914	1	1
1916		1
1919	1	1
1926	1	1
1933	1	
1935	1	1
1940	1	1
1942	1	1
1943	1	
1949	1	1
1950	1	1
1975	1	
1984		1

After Stearns and Macdonald

ABOUT HAWAII'S VOLCANOES

MAUNA LOA

Mauna Loa (long mountain) is the largest single mountain in the world, but most of it is under water. It is more than thirty thousand feet high, measured from the bottom of the ocean. It has been built of an uncountable number of lava flows, each averaging about ten feet thick.

This volcano contains enough rock to make a wall a mile wide and half a mile high around the whole United States.

Mauna Loa is a very active volcano. From 1832 to 1950, it erupted on an average of every three and a half years. From 1950 to 1975 Mauna Loa did not erupt at all.

During the eruption of 1950, the side of the mountain split open for thirteen miles. Melted rock from the cracks flowed in three rivers of lava down the volcano into the sea. The outbreak lasted twenty-three days and poured out enough material to make a four-lane highway, two and a half times around the world. It was one of the largest eruptions of melted rock seen in historic times.

On July 5, 1975, Mauna Loa awakened again after sleeping quietly for twenty-five years. The eruption came with almost no warning at all. No earthquakes were felt and many people slept right through the midnight to morning activity. The fountains up to 150 feet high lighted nearly all of the island of Hawaii. Much of the lava was erupted into craters on the summit, although one *a'a* flow moved about 3 miles down the north slope. As the day progressed, the fountains slowly died away and before dark the eruption had ended.

After a 9 year period of quiet, Mauna Loa once more erupted on March 25, 1984. The activity began on the summit and then cracked out high on the eastern rift, sending several lava flows in an easterly direction. During the next 16 days, lava flows repeatedly advanced toward the city of Hilo, at times coming within 4 miles of the up-slope suburbs.

On March 30, 1984 Kilauea produced the 17th phase of fountaining at Pu'u O. For only the second occasion in history, melted rock gushed from both volcanoes at the same time. In 1868, Mauna Loa and Kilauea erupted simultaneously on their southwest flanks.

After 22 days, the eruption on Mauna Loa ceased, and residents of Hilo relaxed with the feeling that it may be many years before they are again endangered by lava flows from the volcano's east rift zone.

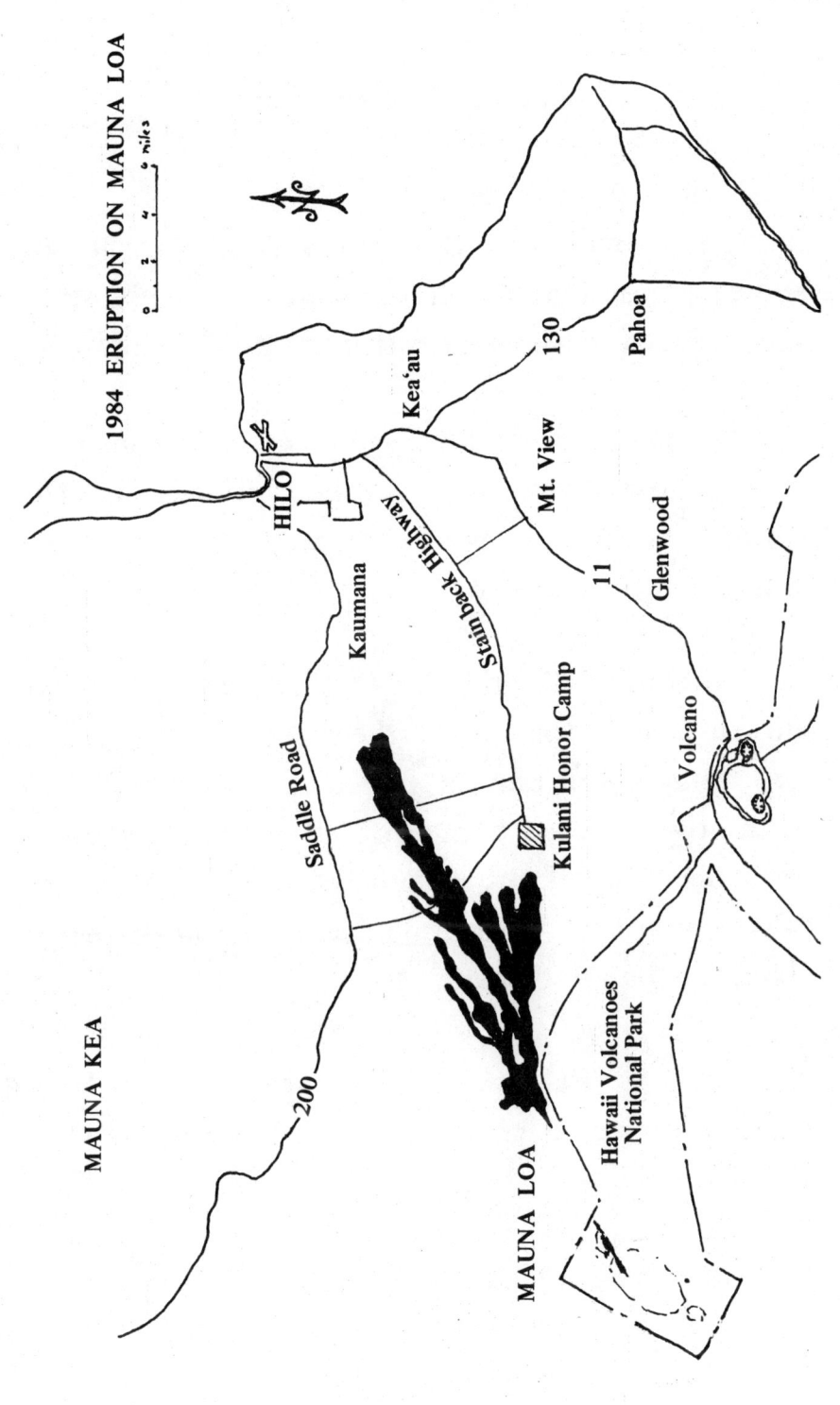

KILAUEA VOLCANO

Compared to Mauna Loa, Kilauea is very small. Its top is only four thousand feet above the sea, and in places it is as flat as a table. In spite of its size, Kilauea is the most active volcano in the world.

The Hawaiians of long ago said that Kilauea had erupted in the time of every king of Hawaii. This volcano is famous for being in almost continual eruption for more than one hundred years.

Between 1823 and 1924, there was a lake of molten lava in the top of the volcano. The melted rock came up in one place, cooled a little, and sank in another place. Sometimes the lake overflowed onto the floor of the caldera. Because of this, the caldera was slowly filled almost five hundred feet in about one hundred years.

In 1924, the lava lake drained away and the volcano exploded. The lava lake never came back to the top of Kilauea.

Since 1961, Kilauea has erupted almost every year, on the side of the volcano along the rift zone.

ABOUT HAWAII'S VOLCANOES

RECENT ACTIVITY

On February 22, 1969, Kilauea erupted along a line between Makaopuhi Crater and Pauahi Crater on the east rift zone. During the following 5 years, the almost continuous eruptive activity built a dome-shaped hill named Mauna Ulu where once was flat, almost level ground. The same fountains up to 1,800 feet high that created the hill and buried Aloi and Alae Craters also sent streams of lava down the cliffs into the sea 7 miles away.

During the period that Mauna Ulu was building and shortly after, Kilauea also experienced eruptions on the summit and the southwest rift zone. On September 13, 1977, the volcano erupted halfway down its east rift zone. The main flow, about 1,000 feet wide, moved toward the village of Kalapana on the coastline. After flowing for one week the lava fanned out and piled up 40 feet thick less than one mile from the village.

The 1979 eruption in the vicinity of Pauahi Crater lasted only a day. Visitors waited in the rain to be driven in to the place where the lava crossed the Chain of Craters Road.

Both of Kilauea's eruptions on 1982 occurred within the caldera. The first on April 30, cracked out just east of Halemaumau in the morning and provided entertainment almost all day. The second on September 25, came without warning and caught geologists by surprise. It began just after sunset inside the southern rim of the caldera and lasted all night to the delight of spectators who watched from the opposite caldera rim only 2 miles away.

The eruption of Kilauea which began on January 3, 1983, cracked out near Napau Crater on the east rift about 7 miles due south of the village of Glenwood. Other fissures opened to the east along a 4 mile length spurting melted rock hundreds of feet into the air at times. Four days later a rapid flow moved down the mountain stopping about 2 miles from the ocean.

On February 14, a vigorous phase of eruptive activity fed a lava stream that flowed 4½ miles southward, ending in a high 300 foot wide wall of a'a that engulfed 2 houses in Royal Gardens near Kalapana before stopping on March 3. Following several brief outbreaks during the month, a strong fountaining phase began on March 28 feeding a flow that moved down the mountain parallel to that of the Valentine's Day phase. Shortly after destroying 4 buildings in Royal Gardens, the phase ended April 6, but the flow continued moving taking 2 more homes.

On June 13 and June 29, 1983, lava flows went down the side of Kilauea into Royal Gardens consuming about 180 lots and 8 houses. Most of the flows during the following 6 months went into the rainforest to the northeast of the source now named Pu'u O, Enduring Hill. During phase 18 which began on April 18, 1984, the subdivision was entered by an a'a flow which destroyed 3 buildings and a pig farm before stopping less than a mile from the ocean.

On November 16, 1983 an earthquake of 6.7 Richter, located on the southwest boundary of Mauna Loa and Kilauea, shook the island of Hawaii, causing extensive damage to roads and homes along a line from Volcano to Hilo. Apparently neither volcano was disturbed internally.

ABOUT HAWAII'S VOLCANOES

THE BIG SHAKE

On November 29, 1975, the largest earthquake in more than a hundred years shook the island of Hawaii. It caused nearly three million dollars in damage, made the volcano of Kilauea erupt and generated a tsunami or tidal wave that took two lives.

Many people on the island of Hawaii were awakened that morning about 3:30 a.m. by a quake of 5.7 intensity that did little or no damge. Because of this there were more observers than usual awake when the big earthquake struck an hour later. This one was measured at 7.2 on the Richter scale. It was felt not only all over the island but as far as the island of Oahu, 250 miles away.

The quake was centered in a sparsely populated area of the southeastern coast line almost 30 miles due south of Hilo. There was extensive minor damage in the downtown portion of the city, in spite of its distance from the epicenter of the earthquake. Waterlines, walls and swimming pools cracked and glass breakage was widespread. Four old houses collapsed and about fifty homes were damaged.

Near the summit of Kilauea the damage was more severe. Roads cracked and buckled, chimneys and water tanks fell and crater walls collapsed. Some roads and trails were so badly damaged that it was necessary to rebuild them elsewhere.

THE ERUPTION

Evidently the earthquake was strong enough to crack the top of the reservoir of Kilauea because almost an hour after the big shake the volcano erupted near the center of the caldera floor.

The first phase of the eruption began with fountains over 150 feet high, playing along a crack more than 500 yards long. This phase produced the most lava although it lasted only an hour and a half. About three hours later the second phase began when a vent opened on the side of Halemaumau Crater, periodically squirting melted rock out onto the crater floor.

Just after dark, following several hours of quiet, the activity resumed at the same vent. This third phase was the most beautiful. Fountains, at times spurting 300 feet high, showered the floor of the crater for more than an hour.

Hilo
Kona
N
MAY 1973
NOV. 1973
NOV. 1979
SEPT. 1971
DEC. 1974
1969-74
0 1 2 miles
KILAUEA ERUPTION MAP
1969 to JUNE 1984
Kalapana
PACIFIC OCEAN

N
PU'U O
NAPAU
KAUKA
HEIHEIAHULU
1977
KILAUEA EAST RIFT ZONE
JUNE 1984
0 1 2 miles
PARK BOUNDARY
Royal Gardens
to Pahoa
NAT'L PARK VISITORS' CENTER
Kaimu
Kalapana
Black Sand Beach
Queen's Bath
PACIFIC OCEAN

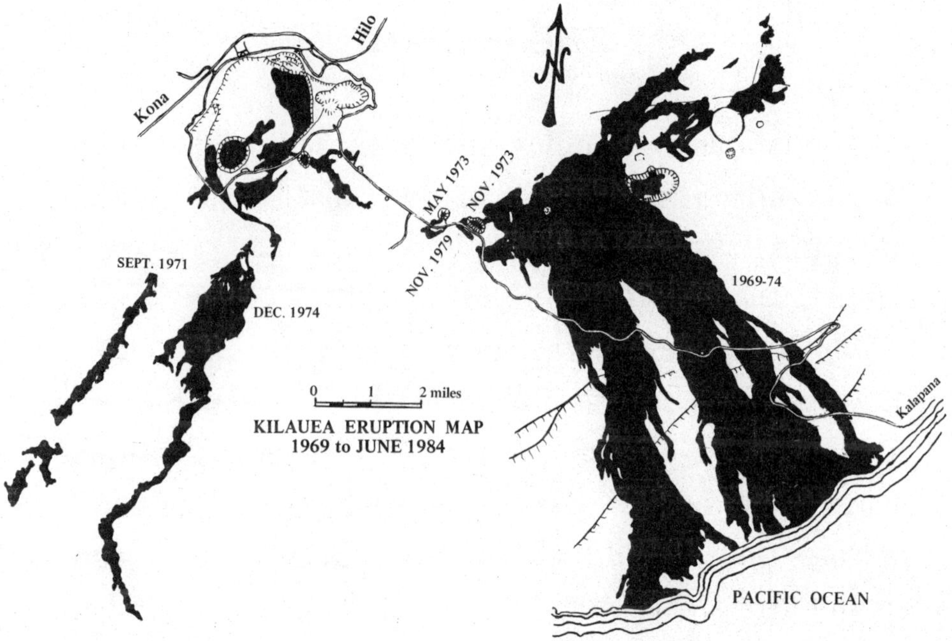

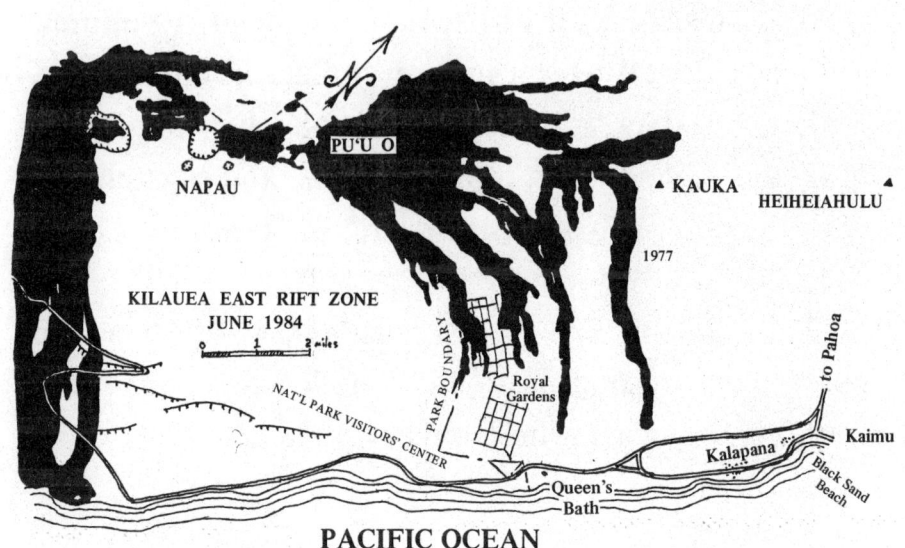

THE TSUNAMI

The tsunami or tidal wave was caused by the abrupt down and out movement of the coast line associated with the huge earthquake.

Probably before the motion of the quake ended the sea began to rise slowly. Within minutes campers at Halape, a coastal retreat in Volcanoes National Park, were swept from their feet by a surging wave. Before they could get their bearings they were engulfed by a larger wave, 50 feet high, that dashed some of them into an old crack in the land, where a succession of waves contined to batter them.

Although the tsunami may have lasted less than ten minutes in all, it left two people dead, 19 injured and caused well over a million dollars in damage. A similar but larger tsunami in 1868 that originated near the same place took 46 lives and wasted the entire southern coast of the island of Hawaii.

The recent big quake caused the southeastern coast line to sink 3 to 12 feet, leaving palm trees standing in the sea where once were beaches.

ABOUT HAWAII'S VOLCANOES

THE LATEST OUTBREAK

After more than 35 months of eruptive activity in the same area, Kilauea still appears to be capable of vigorous behavior. During that period of time, the volcano has had 39 fountaining phases of activity. These geyser-like episodes have lasted from a few hours to several days but during the past year have averaged about 12 hours. Oddly enough, all of the fountains of the past year have lighted the night sky over Kilauea.

No other eruption in historic time has produced so many fountains over 1000 feet high. The fall-out from these geysers of melted rock has built a cone-shaped hill about 800 feet high named Pu'u O, which has become the most prominent feature on Kilauea's upper east rift zone.

Fountaining episodes generally seem to begin in 2 stages. First, melted rock wells up in the principal vent sometimes gushing several yards in the air, creating a glow that can easily be seen for 5 - 10 miles during good weather. This may go on for several days before the vigorous fountain bursts forth in a new phase. Although almost all of the eruptive activity has been confined to Pu'u O vent, some outbreaks have occurred in fissures nearby that have lasted more than 2 weeks.

Kilauea has been quite active during 1985. As of December 1st the volcano has had 11 fountaining phases in 11 months. While May and August had no visual activity, June and September each had 2 such periods.

While the 17th phase of fountaining was going on at Pu'u O on Kilauea's east rift on March 30, 1984, Mauna Loa volcano also erupted on its east rift above Hilo. This made only the second time in history that both Mauna Loa and Kilauea erupted at the same time. Although lava flows from Mauna Loa came within 4 miles of Hilo, no structures were harmed by them.

ABOUT HAWAII'S VOLCANOES

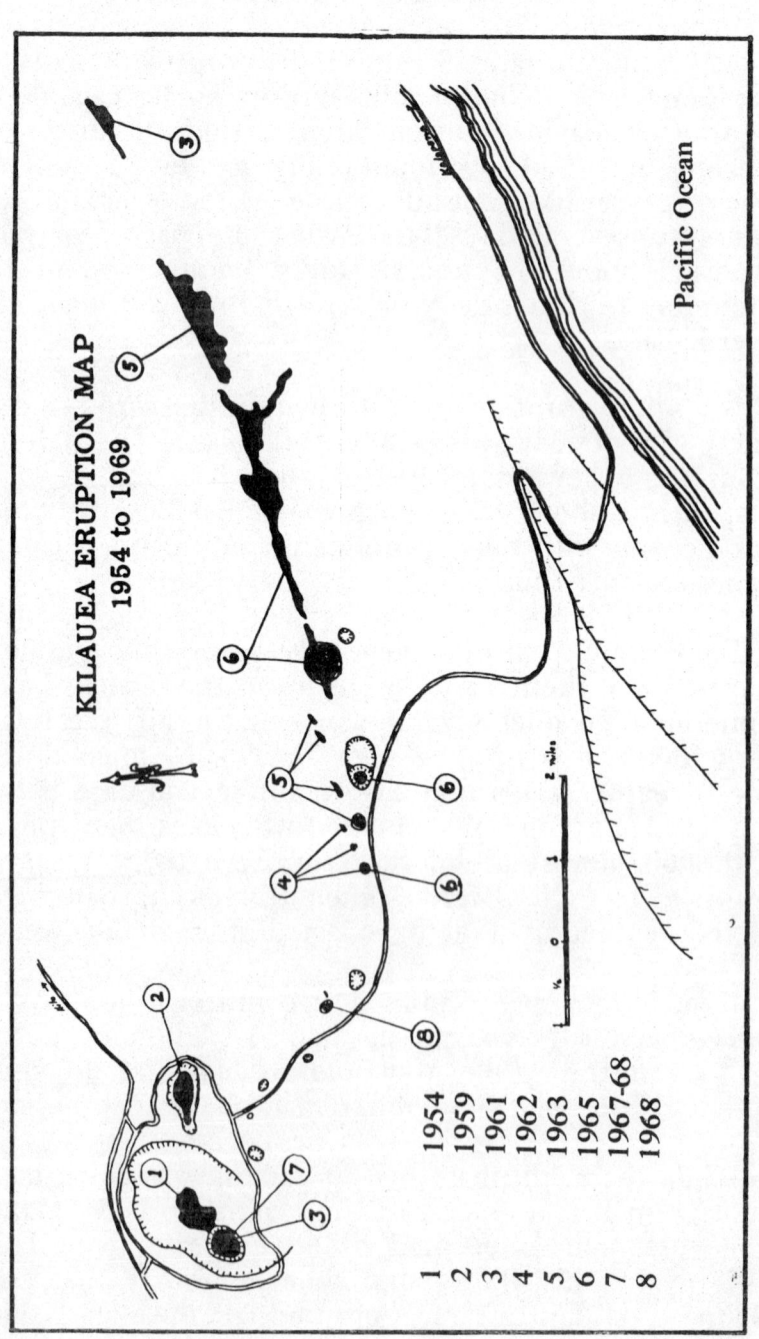

ABOUT HAWAII'S VOLCANOES 31

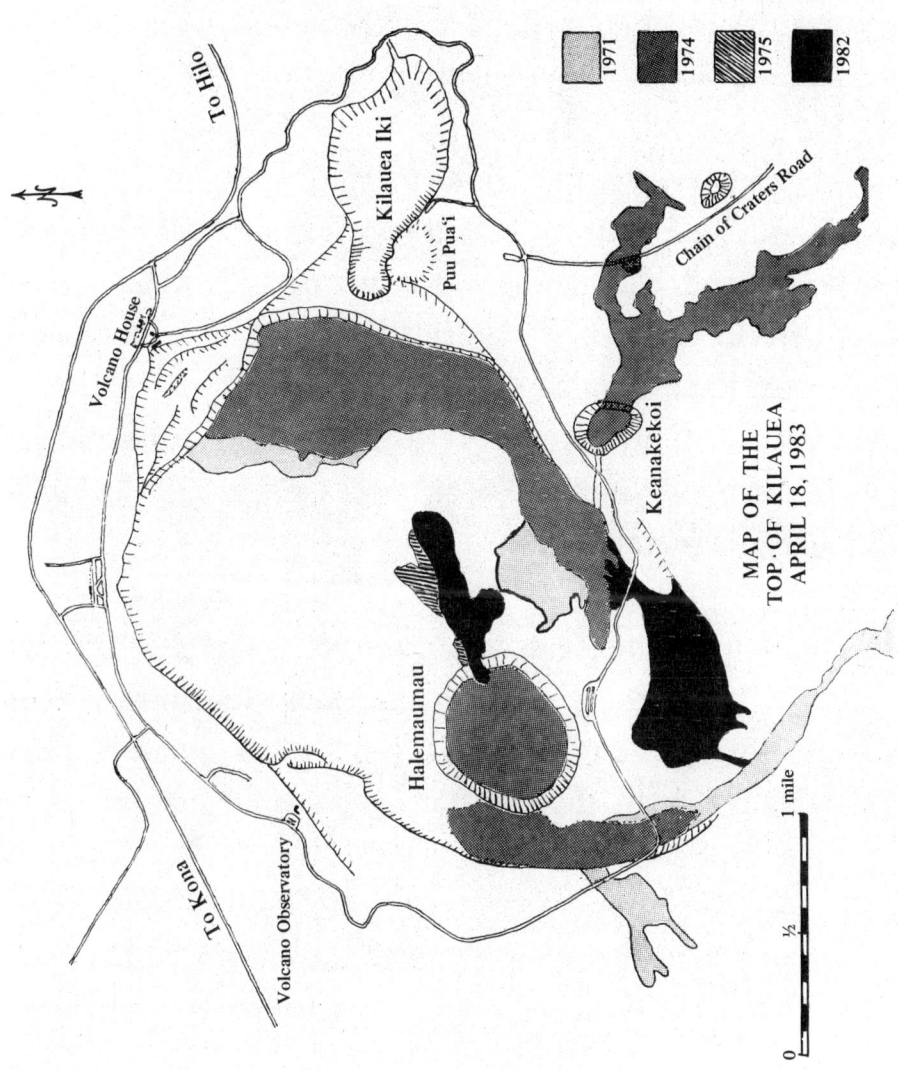

MAP OF THE
TOP OF KILAUEA
APRIL 18, 1983

KILAUEA IKI CRATER

Kilauea Iki means little Kilauea. It is a large crater on the top of Kilauea Volcano. Only a wall of old lava stands like a dam between the crater and the caldera.

After two small eruptions in 1832 and 1868, Kilauea Iki was quiet for a long time. Trees had covered the floor, and there was a hiking trail through them. Then, in October of 1959, thousands of earthquakes shook the volcano. The walls of the crater cracked the next month, and an eruption began. The highest fountain of melted rock ever measured occurred during this eruption.

At one time, the lava fountain roared 1900 feet into the air; more than five hundred feet higher that the Empire State Building. Scientists measured the temperature of the fountain and found it to be more than 2000 degrees.

Melted rock falling from the fountain built a new hill on the rim of the crater. It was named *Puu Pua'i*, the thrown-up hill.

When the eruption was over the crater floor was covered by a cooling lava lake 380 feet deep.

ABOUT HAWAII'S VOLCANOES

HALEMAUMAU

The crater inside the caldera of Kilauea is called Halemaumau. Visitors seldom realize, as they stand at the edge of this crater, that they are almost a tenth of a mile down inside the most active volcano in the world.

Years ago, the Hawaiians said that in this place were two craters. One had *amaumau* ferns growing all over its sloping sides. It was named Halemaumau-Fern House. The other crater had steep walls on which nothing grew. It was called *Ka Lua O Pele* - The Pit of Pele. This was the home of the goddess of the volcanoes.

About 1790, the volcano exploded and made one big crater where the two were before. Sometime after that, a bubbling lava lake rose in the crater and lasted over a hundred years. In 1924, the melted rock drained away and the volcano exploded again, making the crater the size it is today.

Halemaumau is now about half a mile across and about three hundred feet deep. It is seldom the same for very long.

34 ABOUT HAWAII'S VOLCANOES

Halemaumau

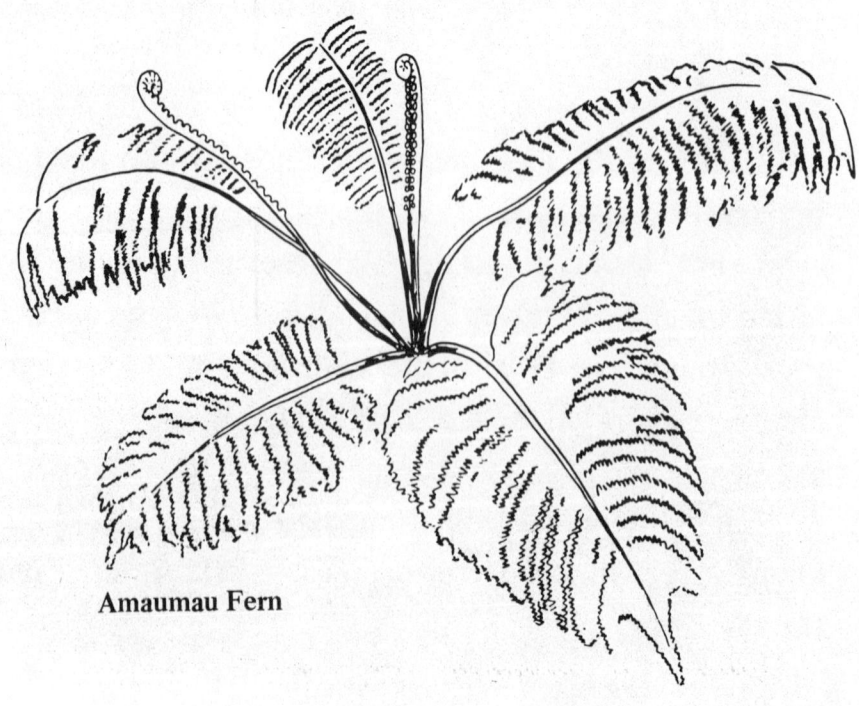

Amaumau Fern

ABOUT HAWAII'S VOLCANOES

KILAUEA ERUPTIONS

From 1823 to 1924 there was an almost continuous eruption on the top of the mountain.

YEAR	ON MOUNTAIN TOP		ON SIDE
1924	STEAM EXPLOSION	CALDERA	
1924	1	CALDERA	
1927	1	HALEMAUMAU	
1929	2	HALEMAUMAU	
1930	1	HALEMAUMAU	
1931	1	HALEMAUMAU	
1934	1	HALEMAUMAU	
1952	1	HALEMAUMAU	
1954	1	CALDERA	
1955			1
1959	1	KILAUEA IKI	
1960			1
1961	3	HALEMAUMAU	1
1962			1
1963			2
1965			2
1967	1	HALEMAUMAU	
1968			2
1969*			2
1971		CALDERA	1
1973			2
1974	1	HALEMAUMAU	
1974	1	SUMMIT	1
1975	1	CALDERA	
1977			1
1979			1
1982	2		
1983			1
1984	(Eruption continuing in 1984.)		1

* The second eruption lasted more than five years.

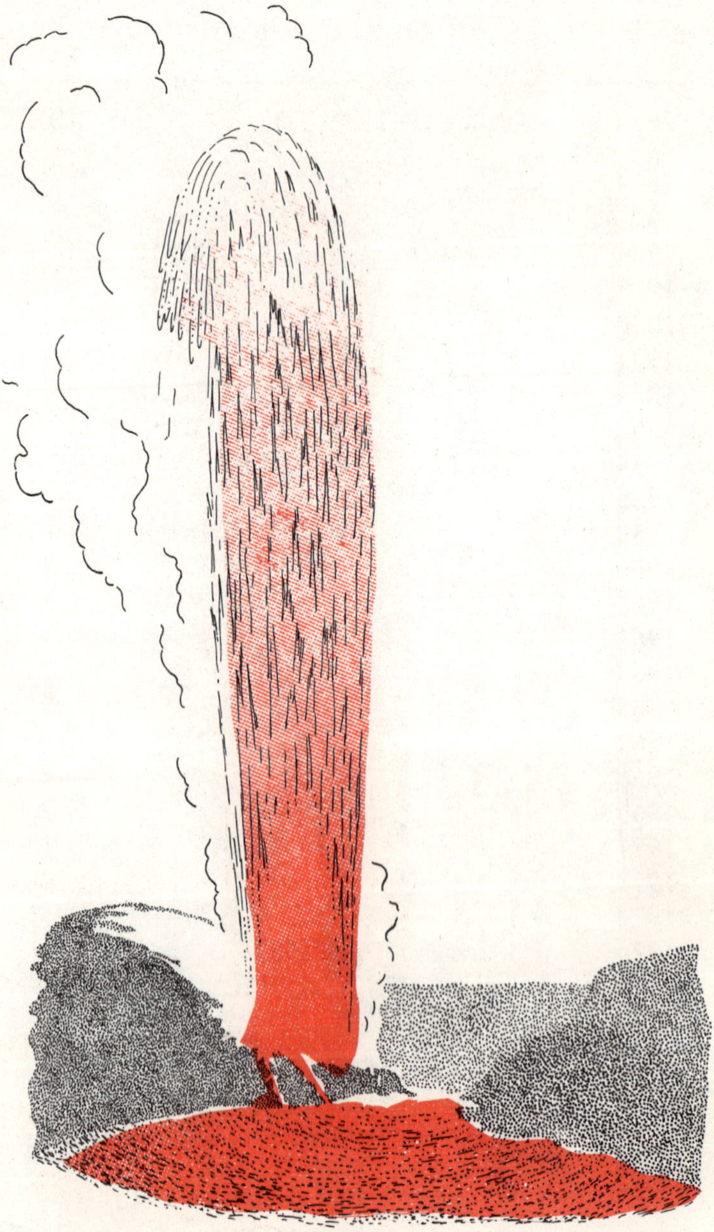

THE HAWAIIAN VOLCANO OBSERVATORY

On the highest edge of Kilauea Caldera is the Hawaiian Volcano Observatory. Here, the scientists from the U.S. Geological Survey have kept constant watch on the volcanoes since 1912. The scientists observe and keep records on all eruptions as they are happening. They take the temperature of lava fountains and measure how high they are. They photograph eruptions from the ground and from planes and are able to warn people of dangerous lava flows.

When the volcanoes are quiet, the scientists are still busy taking the temperature of lava lakes, measuring the swelling of the volcano, and counting the earthquakes that are recorded.

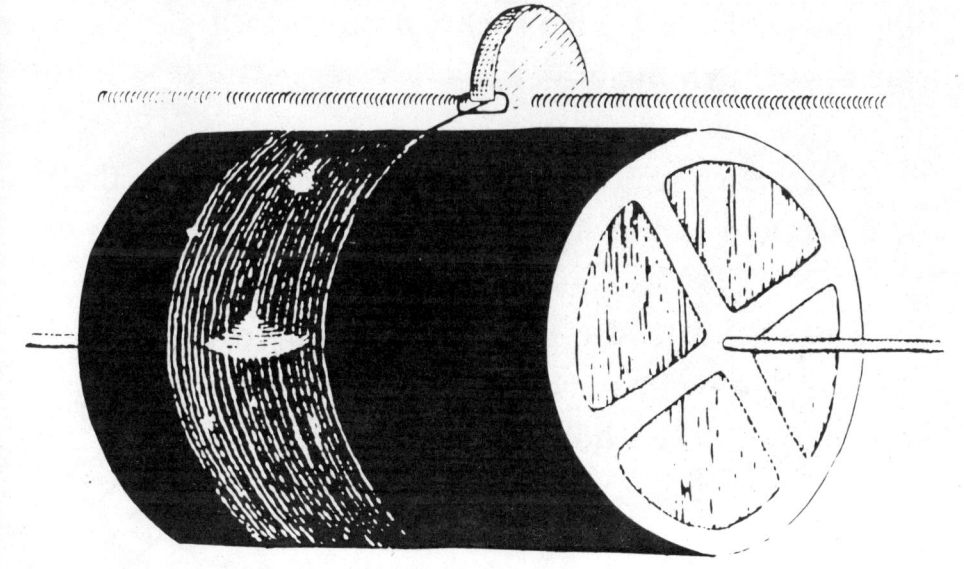

TAKING A VOLCANO'S TEMPERATURE

Taking the temperature of erupting lava could be hard to do. It is very dangerous to get too close to a fountain of melted rock shooting hundreds of feet high.

Scientists have a way of measuring temperature from a safe distance. They know that a very hot thing glows and changes color as it heats. First it gets red, then orange, then yellow, and sometimes nearly white.

The scientists look at the fountain through a optical pyrometer. It looks like a small telescope with changeable colored pieces inside. He matches the color of the melted rock with a colored piece in the optical pyrometer.

Since each color has a certain temperature the scientist knows how hot the fountain is.

The scientists also take the temperature of a lava lake as the melted rock cools. They use a drilling machine to make a hole in the crust.

ABOUT HAWAII'S VOLCANOES

HOW A SEISMOGRAPH WORKS

A bucket with a pencil fastened to the bottom makes a very simple earthquake detector or seismograph.

When the bucket is hung on a chain and filled with lead, it is so heavy that it is hard to move even by shaking the chain. A sheet of paper fastened to the floor so the pencil tip just touches it is the record or seismogram.

When an earthquake comes, the bucket of lead is slow to move but the floor under it is not. The bucket nearly stands still while the floor shakes, marking the paper with pencil lines.

Modern seismographs are far more sensitive. They record on a sheet of smoked paper that is fastened to a turning drum. Every day the old paper is taken off and a new one put on.

During a quiet day on Kilauea volcano, the seismographs record about fifty earthquakes. These are caused by rock splitting or slipping inside the volcano. Most of the earthquakes are too small for people to feel.

Another kind of motion recorded by the seismograph is called harmonic tremor. This is a vibration like the one you feel when you put your hand on a water pipe or hose and someone turns on the water.

It is caused by the melted rock moving through cracks or holes inside the volcano. When harmonic tremor is recorded for several hours without stopping, the scientists look for an eruption anytime.

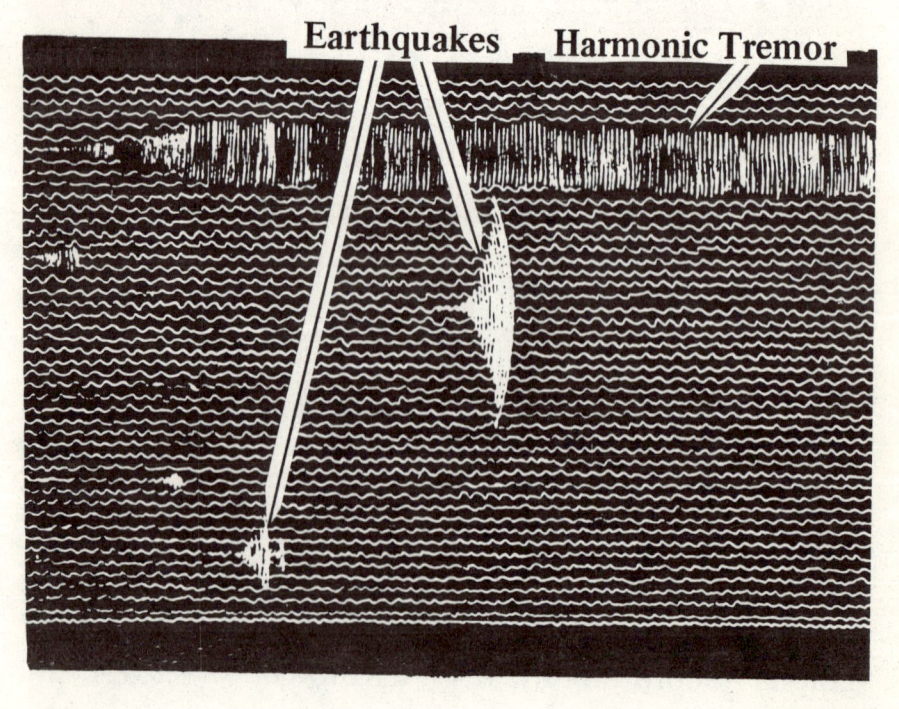

ABOUT HAWAII'S VOLCANOES

WHEN IS THE NEXT ERUPTION?

This question is often asked by visitors. Telling when a volcano will erupt is hard to do. Sometimes eruptions come without warning. At other times there are thousands of earthquakes and no eruption.

Scientists believe they can tell when the volcanoes are able to erupt. They measure the swelling of the mountain top every day as the reservoir below fills with melted rock. They do this by reading a very accurate level, something like the one a carpenter uses, but a hundred times longer.

This water level is called a tilt meter. It is so sensitive that if one end of a bridge six miles long was lifted high enough to put a nickel under it, the tilt meter could tell how much the bridge was tipped.

A volcano sometimes slowly swells up until its top is several feet higher than usual. When it does this the scientists think the volcano may erupt at any time.

EXPLOSIVE ERUPTIONS

Certain things have to happen before a Hawaiian volcano can explode in a steam eruption. That is why this seldom takes place.

The melted rock in the reservoir has to drain away. An eruption under the ocean surface can do this. Then a crack has to open in the volcano to let the sea water into the reservoir.

Because the reservoir is still very hot, the water is changed to steam. Then the steam roars out of a crack or crater, throwing rocks and dust thousands of feet into the air.

Kilauea is the only Hawaiian volcano that has exploded in historic time. In 1790, part of a Hawaiian army was killed by a steam explosion from Halemaumau.

Again in 1924 a small steam eruption killed one man. The caldera floor around Halemaumau is covered with rocks that fell from that eruption.

FOSSILS

Of course there are no dinosaur bones or tracks in Hawaii. The islands are too new. Some of the oldest bones found are those of a goose. The bird was buried by the dust of a steam explosion ten thousand years ago.

When a *pahoehoe* lava flow moves through a forest, it often leaves fossils behind. As it flows around the trees, a thin layer hardens quickly around each tree. Although the lava is hard, it is still hot enough to burn up the tree inside. This leaves a hole, called a tree mold, where the tree was.

If the *pahoehoe* flows around the trees and then drains away, the tree trunks are coated with a layer of rock. The trees burn, leaving high hollow rocks like chimneys standing in a field of lava. These are called lava trees.

Mud from steam explosions has made fossils of leaves, ferns and even footprints. The army caught in the eruption of 1790 left their tracks. You can still see them and the track of a pig in the National Park.

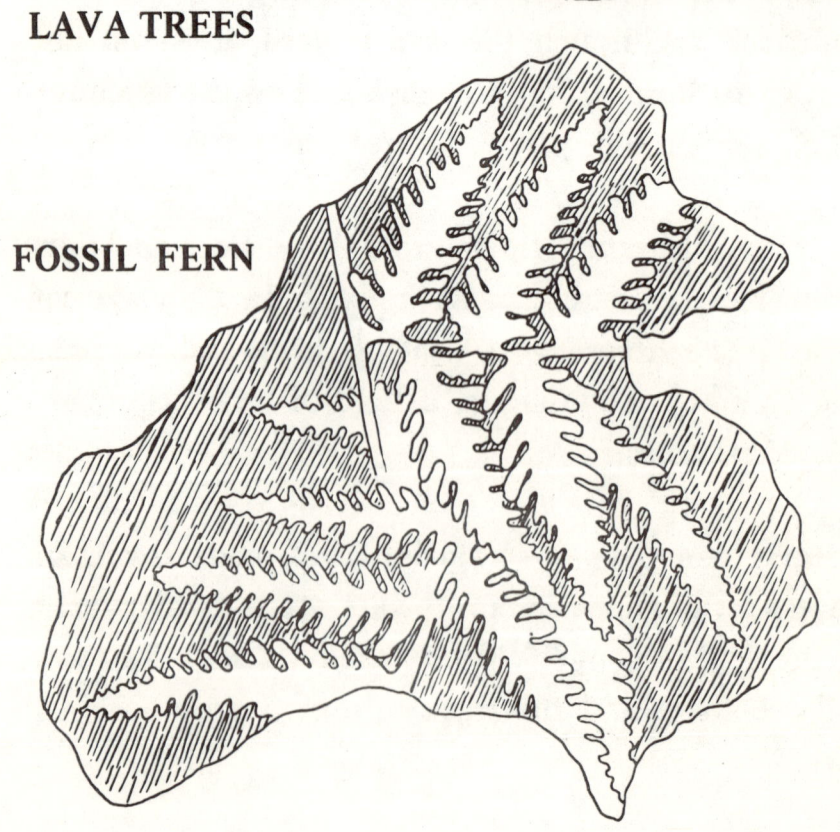

LAVA TREES

FOSSIL FERN

ABOUT HAWAII'S VOLCANOES

HAWAII VOLCANOES NATIONAL PARK

The top of Mauna Loa and a large part of Kilauea are in Hawaii Volcanoes National Park.

In 1916, the people of the United States set aside this land as a National Park so that it would not be changed. Today, most of it is just as the Hawaiian of ancient times knew it.

Much of the park can be seen from a car, but there are many trails for horses and hiking. One can walk across the caldera of Kilauea or down into a crater. There are hills, cliffs, and forests to enjoy.

Visitors can see free movies of volcano eruptions at the Visitor Center every day. A Park Ranger will answer questions about the volcanoes and the park.

Thousands of people come to Hawaii Volcanoes National Park when Kilauea erupts. Park Rangers permit them to get as close as is safe to the eruption fountains. They also explain what is happening, so that no one will be afraid.

MAP OF MAUI

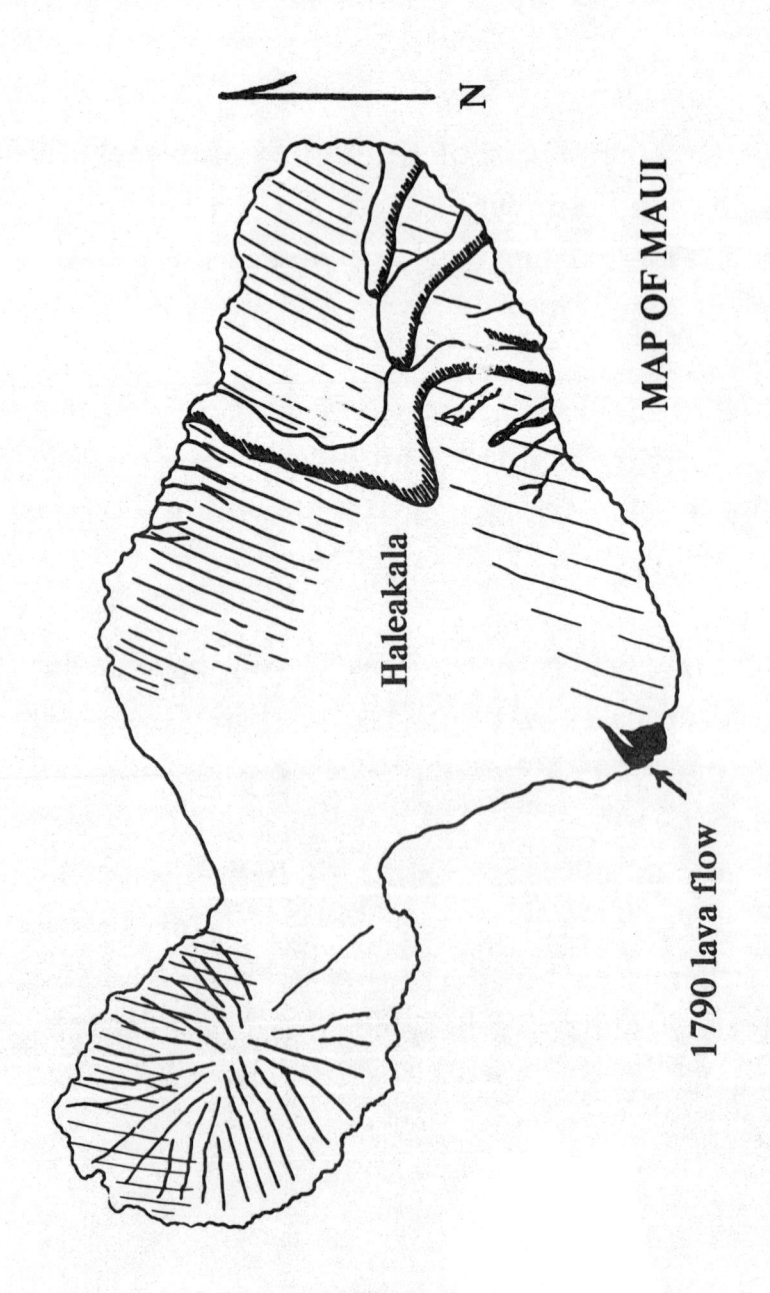

Haleakala

1790 lava flow

ABOUT HAWAII'S VOLCANOES

HALEAKALA VOLCANO

Maui is the island north of Hawaii. The eastern part of it is a large volcano called Haleakala (the house of the sun). An old story tells of a Hawaiian boy named Maui who climbed this mountain to catch the sun with a rope. The top of Haleakala is also a National Park.

Haleakala is a very old volcano. It is so old that the deep valleys cut into its sides have come together on top. They make a very large flat hole that looks something like a caldera. It has big pink and brown cinder cones all over the floor.

Although Haleakala is probably older than Mauna Kea on Hawaii, it still is an active volcano. The last eruption happened about 1790. The melted rock came out of the side of the volcano and poured into the ocean near the south end of the island.

PELE, THE VOLCANO GODDESS

According to Hawaii's legends, Pele was a stranger with pale skin who came to Hawaii in olden times and stayed to become the goddess of volcanoes.

Before that time, there was a volcano god. His name was Ai Laau (forest eater). He was a poor god and also a coward. When he heard that Pele had come to the island, he ran away and never came back.

Then Pele climbed Kilauea and dug a crater with a magic digging stick. She made her home in Halemaumau, and each time that she showed herself the volcano erupted.

The stories say that on top of the volcano Pele was young and beautiful. When she moved underground and came out on the side of the mountains, she was old and ugly.

Although most people in Hawaii today do not believe in Pele, they still like to hear the old stories of the volcano goddess.

ABOUT HAWAII'S VOLCANOES   49

In one of the stories Pele met a man named Kamapuaa (pig child). He was brought back from a far away land by Chief Olopana, a famous Hawaiian sailor.

Kamapuaa wore the skin of a pig and could change into a pig whenever he wanted to. He could also change into other things.

He and Pele were married for a while, but then started to fight. Kamapuaa said Pele was always angry. Pele said he was dirty as a pig.

Kamapuaa brought heavy rain to put out Pele's fire in Halemaumau. Pele threw melted rock at him. For a while, Kamapuaa seemed to be winning. Then Pele directed a lava flow toward him and Kamapuaa was burned. He changed to other things that he might get away. First he became a pig, then ferns, then grass, and, finally, a tiny fish called a hog fish.

After that, these were the items that the people offered to Pele when they wanted to please her. The gifts showed Pele that they were on her side.

ABOUT THE MT. SAINT HELENS ERUPTION

The recent eruptions of Mt. St. Helens in Washington have prompted the question, "Could it happen here?". The answer is "probably not" because the volcanoes in Hawaii are completely different.

Mt. St. Helens and other similar volcanoes differ mainly in the composition of the melt they produce. The melted rock in these continental volcanoes contains as much as 92% to 96% silica. (Mt. Pelee in Martinique once extruded a huge spine of pure silica.)

The more silica added to a melt the thicker and more viscous it becomes, and thus is able to contain the gasses mixed with it until they reach explosive potential. The eruption of a continental volcano may be extremely violent, sending a cloud of incandescent foam sweeping down the mountainside. At the same time the expanding gasses within the cloud add to its speed which may reach well over 200 miles an hour. This great force and tremendous heat often destroy all life in their path.

By contrast, oceanic volcanoes such as Kilauea and Mauna Loa produce melted rock containing less than 50% silica. At a similar temperature the melted rock remains thinner and more fluid, permitting the gasses inside to escape easily. As the gasses effervesce they squirt the melted rock high in the air in a beautiful display.

The few explosive events that have occurred on Hawaii's volcanoes have apparently been the result of steam filling the reservoir following an eruption of lava under the sea. Only two relatively mild steam eruptions have happened in Hawaii in historic time. Both were observed by a multitude of people only a mile or two from the main vent.